READING &WRITING

WITH

LETTERLAND

A PARENT'S GUIDE

BY
JUDY MANSON

LETTERLAND
Direct

Published by
LETTERLAND DIRECT LIMITED
P.O. Box 161
Leatherhead
Surrey KT23 3YB

© Letterland Direct Limited 1992
Revised edition 1993

Letterland® was devised by and
is the copyright of Lyn Wendon

With thanks to all the children and teachers
who provided illustrations for this book

ISBN 1 85834 101 9
Printed and bound in the United Kingdom

Edited by Richard Carlisle and Stephanie Laslett

Designed by FdK Design Consultants

CONTENTS

FOREWORD *by Lyn Wendon, originator of Letterland*

Parents are becoming increasingly interested in how their children learn to read. Literacy skills are the foundation of a child's every other future attainment, so it becomes a great help to the children when parents and teachers join together to support their reading, writing and spelling.

To explain the complexities of written English, with its many rules and even more exceptions, at a child's level of interest is quite challenging. I have chosen to explain it in a language of childhood to reach children of all abilities. A whole network of little stories from a secret place where letters live, called Letterland, makes it easy for children to understand how the alphabet is constructed.

These stories explain what sounds to associate with each letter and how changes in letter behaviour within words can be predicted (yes, predicted). By interacting with the Letterland characters and stories, children become confident in handling this new, more friendly world of print.

You are likely to find your child coming home from school or kindergarten wanting to tell you the latest item learned about Letterland – that is, about reading! This means that he or she will be talking about the Hairy Hat Man, or Annie Apple, or Clever Cat, or Poor Peter... or any of the other characters in Letterland. What are you, poor parent, to make of it all? You were never taught this way and here you are, expected to know what your child is talking about!

This is where the PARENT'S GUIDE comes in. A very experienced Letterland teacher, Judy Manson, sets out for you the principles of Letterland and introduces you to its characters.

To the children it is all play and fantasy, but you will know how the fantasy translates into the facts of literacy. You will be able to see how, as a result, the mysteries of print will yield to familiarity and understanding.

Join in. When you and your child share the Letterland secrets you'll both have a great time – and you will probably learn more than you expected about your own language.

■ INTRODUCTION

Most of us remember very little about how we learned to read. It comes as a shock to discover through our children, as they struggle to master print, how complicated letters and words can be. There is a lot of difficult information for them to learn and much of it is of little interest to a 4, 5 or 6 year old!

This book is about learning to read and write with Letterland. It is also about how you can help your child, both before school age and once your child is at school. It does not set out to turn you into a teacher, but rather to inform you in a helper's role, so that any help you give is as useful as possible.

One of the secrets of Letterland's success is that this imaginary place makes it possible to teach all the difficult information about written language through stories. These stories entertain children as they carry home the information. No boring rules and exceptions. Instead Letterland characters like Annie Apple, Bouncy Ben and Clever Cat

make children aware of the sounds letters make, and show how letters interact with each other in predictable ways.

By learning "who's who" in Letterland, and knowing some of the stories, you can offer consistent support to your child.

Letterland teaching is entirely consistent with the Attainment Targets of the National Curriculum (outlined at the back of this book) and fits in with any Reading Scheme. It has already proved its worth in thousands of schools, among hundreds of thousands of children.

Now it is *your* turn to discover Letterland, and the ways in which it can help your child on the road to successful reading and writing.

Merland Rise First School, Epsom

LEARNING TO READ AND WRITE

Most adult memories of learning to read and write revolve around reciting the alphabet, parrot fashion. Children learning with Letterland are more fortunate. The Letterland characters bring the alphabet to life, and make the job of mastering letters and words a pleasure!

Learning to read and write is one of the most demanding things children ever do. To appreciate the difficulty children face, imagine *you* were trying to learn the Arabic alphabet. Look at the Arabic word for 'bread' shown below. Each dash or dot has a

significant position. Indeed, many would argue that Arabic is easier to learn than English, because each letter shape has a corresponding, unchanging sound. In our language, the letters change their sound often!

Think about our alphabet – the "aee, bee, cee". Learning these alphabet names will not give the young child much help because not one of the 21 consonant names is ever used in reading. Three-quarters of all the consonants actually begin with another letter's sound. H "aitch" never says **a** or **ch**. W "double-you" never says **d** or **y** or **u**. No wonder children find these early steps such a struggle.

Letterland is based on important phonic principles. This means that it builds on the sound of each letter – the actual sound it makes in a word. Character names like Annie Apple, Bouncy Ben and Clever Cat are more effective than "aee, bee, cee" because the sound is *always at the start* of the name. Letterland's main strength is the way in which it makes these letters come alive.

Look at the letter **h**. To a young child coming to our alphabet for the first time there are no clues within this letter's shape or in its name to the sound it makes in words. But if **h** becomes the Hairy Hat Man, both his body shape and his name become steady clues, putting the correct **hhh** sound on the child's lips the moment he or she starts to name him: "**Hhh**airy **Hhh**at Man". Meaningless symbols become children's friends.

By using character names instead of the alphabet names, Letterland enables you and your child to talk about any letter without risk of confusion. A child can easily confuse "ess" with "cee", but when you both talk about Sammy Snake and Clever Cat each of you will always know exactly which letter you mean.

The English language is complex and contradictory. No sooner have you learnt a letter sound than it turns up in different words making a completely different sound. Your child masters this new quirk and then discovers the same letter does something entirely new when in a different combination of letters. Look at the letter **e**.

Listen to its sound in these words:

p**e**a	p**e**rson
p**e**t	**e**ight
pi**e**	h**e**ight
p**e**ar	fi**e**rce

Confused? If *you* are, think how easily children are confused. Letters behave in this unpredictable way all the time, especially the vowels: **a**, **e**, **i**, **o** and **u**.

Every word has at least one vowel in it! So how can you begin to explain the logic behind the strange rules that govern the English language?

In Letterland, the explanations are given by means of simple stories about what happens when particular letters get together. The stories provide reasons why letters sometimes change their sounds. Something a child can grasp and remember. For example, why do **s** and **h** make a **sh** sound?

This is the Letterland story. "Sammy Snake is a noisy letter, always hissing in words, but Hairy Hat Man is always quiet (he even walks into words bare-footed so that the sound of his footsteps won't stop us from hearing his quiet, whispered **hhh** sound). But when you see Sammy Snake next to the Hairy Hat Man in a word, he is busy hushing Sammy Snake up like this, "**sh**!", because the Hairy Hat Man hates noise."

Ask yourself what you still remember from your childhood. Nursery rhymes and fairy stories, or mathematical equations? Research has shown that we are better able to retain information in the form of a story than as a series of rules, symbols or numbers. For example, memory experts use story "maps" to memorise long sequences of letters or numbers, recalling them perfectly weeks later.

A simple story is eagerly accepted by the child and, improbable though the explanation may seem to you, to a child the logic behind the

Letterland characters' behaviour is clear. "Now I know why you can't hear the **h** in w**h**y, w**h**ich and w**h**ere," your child may come home from school and tell you. "The Water Witch* is cross because she can't see the way ahead with the Hairy Hat Man standing in front of her – he's so tall. So she knocks his hat off. That makes him too surprised to speak."

The Letterland witch is mischievous, not evil. Children love to outwit her.

Your child will find it easier to share stories like these with you if you have some foreknowledge of how Letterland teaching works. Otherwise you may just laugh and dismiss the conversation as unimportant. Your encouragement is important in helping to build your child's confidence.

WHO'S WHO IN

Annie Apple

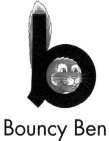
Bouncy Ben

Clever Cat

Golden Girl

Hairy Hat Man

Impy Ink

Munching Mike

Naughty Nick

Oscar Orange

Sammy Snake

Ticking Tess

Uppy Umbrella

Vase of Violets

THE VOWEL MEN

Mr A

Mr E

LETTERLAND

Dippy Duck

Eddy Elephant

Fireman Fred

Jumping Jim

Kicking King

Lamp Lady

Poor Peter

Quarrelsome Queen

Robber Red

Wicked Water Witch

Kissing Cousins

Yo-Yo Man

Zig Zag Zebra

Mr I

Mr O

Mr U

STARTING WITH LETTERLAND

Children often begin to show an interest in letters and words at the pre-school stage. Many parents are keen to encourage this curiosity but find they soon come up against problems. How to explain, for example, that letters make different sounds; what to call the letters and how to pronounce and write them correctly. Most important of all, how to ensure that their child doesn't lose interest. You will find that Letterland excites the child's imagination – and provides practical help with every aspect of reading and writing.

■ STARTING TO READ

Let's try to enter the world of print with a child's inexperienced eye. Try to forget that we have had twenty or more years' practice at deciphering printed words. Look at these cat pictures.

Each cat is slightly different but in a story book a young child would recognise each one as a cat. The differences do not change the meaning of the lines that form the image.

Now look at the letters

b d p and **q**.

In each letter, the small differences change the letter completely. These small differences are also a feature of words. Compare the words

bib did pip

or the more common words

was saw

in is it.

Every slight change makes an important difference.

In the Letterland system each letter becomes a unique character. Each is a person or animal with a personality all its own. The illustration fused with the letter is its **picture code**. Each letter shape is picture coded and is given a personal name.

Here the letter **a** is picture coded to become **Annie Apple**.

Because the round apple is placed right inside the round **a** shape, the picture clue and the letter shape become fixed together in the child's mind.

The letter's sound is always on the child's lips when starting to say its Letterland name: **A**nnie **A**pple – ă. The picture coding helps the child to map on to the letter shape and distinguish it from a similar letter shape.

Now look at the Letterland **b d p q**.

Once children have looked at these picture coded letters, they are able to see the plain letter shapes in a new light.

| Bouncy Ben | Dippy Duck | Poor Peter | Quarrelsome Queen |

When they learn to picture code the letters themselves, by adding ears, whiskers or a tail for example, they will strengthen their new way of "seeing". Rather than asking your child to ring all the "dee's" in this group of letters, it is much more fun to ask, "Spot Dippy Duck's letter wherever you can find it, and draw on her head and tail feathers."

d   b   p   d   p

b   p   d   b   d

p   d   b   d   b

PRONOUNCING THE LETTERS

The Consonants

It will help your child if you are able to pronounce each letter correctly. The most common mistake in pronouncing letters is to add the "uh" sound to a letter.

To make the correct sound, start to say the character name. By adding "uh" we make an impure sound. No wonder when children sound out the word **but** as "buh-uh-tuh" they assume the word is "butter!"

Stop your voice short after these letters:

b..., **d**..., **g**..., **j**..., **y**

These are the hardest letter sounds to make without adding any "uh" sound.

The dreaded "uh" sound is easy to avoid, however, with all the following letters. Just whisper them!

c, **fff**, **hhh**, **k**, **p**, **sss**,

t, and **x** (whisper ks).

The trick for avoiding "uh" with the next group of letters is simply to prolong them and keep your jaw closed at the end.

lll..., **mmm**..., **nnn**..., **rrr**..., **vvv**..., **www**..., **yyy**..., and **zzz**...

The Vowels

The vowels **a**, **e**, **i**, **o** and **u** are more difficult because vowels make both short and long sounds, depending on the word.

The *first* most useful sound to teach for the five vowels is the "short" sound. This is the sound you hear at the start of each Letterland character name.

| Annie | Eddy | Impy | Oscar | Uppy |
| Apple | Elephant | Ink | Orange | Umbrella |

Next comes the "long" sound – picture coded in Letterland as the Vowel Men. These are the only inhabitants of Letterland who ever say their alphabet names in words, and then only at special times – but more about that later. So Mr A says "aee", Mr E says "eee", Mr I says "iee", Mr O says "oh", Mr U says "yoo".

Mr A   Mr E   Mr I   Mr O   Mr U

HOW TO PRONOUNCE

 Annie Apple makes the sound at the beginning of her name – ă (as in ăpple).

 Bouncy Ben makes the sound at the beginning of his name – **b**. Stop your voice right after **b**. Don't add "uh".

Clever Cat makes the sound at the beginning of her name – **c**. Just whisper it.

 Golden Girl makes the sound at the beginning of her name – **g**. Stop your voice right after **g**. Don't add "uh".

 Hairy Hat Man makes the sound at the beginning of his name – **h**. Just whisper it – **hhh**.

 Impy Ink makes the sound at the beginning of his name – **i** (as in ĭnk).

 Munching Mike makes the sound at the beginning of his name – **m**. Keep your mouth closed and hum – **mmm**. Don't add "uh".

 Naughty Nick makes the sound at the beginning of his name – **n.** Keep your jaw nearly closed, lips open – **nnn**. Don't add "uh".

 Oscar Orange makes the sound at the beginning of his name – ŏ (as in ŏrange).

Sammy Snake makes the sound at the beginning of his name – **s**. Just whisper **sss**.

 Ticking Tess makes the sound at the beginning of her name – **t**. Just whisper it.

 Uppy Umbrella makes the sound at the beginning of her name – ŭ (as in ŭmbrella). For once "uh" is right!

 Vase of Violets makes the sound at the beginning of their name – **v**. Keep your jaw nearly closed – **vvv**. Don't add "uh".

GUIDANCE:
The only letters that ever say their traditional alphabet names in words are the five Vowel Men, Mr A, Mr E, Mr I, Mr O and Mr U.

THE VOWEL MEN

 Mr A, The Apron Man, says his name **A** as in **a**pron.

 Mr E, The Easy Magic Man, says his name **E** as in **e**asy.

THE LETTERS

 Dippy Duck makes the sound at the beginning of her name – **d**. Stop your voice right after **d**. Don't add "uh".

 Eddy Elephant makes the sound at the beginning of his name – **ĕ** (as in **ĕ**lephant).

 Fireman Fred makes the sound at the beginning of his name – **f.** Just whisper it – **fff**.

 Jumping Jim makes the sound at the beginning of his name – **j**. Stop your voice right after **j**. Don't add "uh".

 Kicking King makes the sound at the beginning of his name – **k**. Just whisper it.

 Lamp Lady Lucy makes the sound at the beginning of her name – **lll**. Keep your jaw nearly closed as you make her sound. Don't add "uh".

 Poor Peter makes the sound at the beginning of his name – **p**. Just whisper it.

 Quarrelsome Queen makes the sound at the beginning of her name – **q**. Whisper "kw".

 Robber Red makes the sound at the beginning of his name – **r**. Keep your jaw closed and prolong his sound – **rrr**. Don't add "uh".

 Wicked Water Witch makes the sound at the beginning of her name – **w**. Get ready to whistle but instead just blow **www**. Don't add "uh".

 Max and Maxine, the Kissing Cousins, make the sound **ks**. Just whisper it.

 Yo-Yo Man makes the sound at the beginning of his name – **y**. Keep your jaw nearly closed – **yyy**. Don't add "uh".

 Zig Zag Zebra makes the sound at the beginning of her name – **z**. Keep your jaw nearly closed – **zzz**. Don't add "uh".

 Mr I, The Ice Cream Man, says his name **I** as in **i**ce cream.

 Mr O, The Old Man from over the Ocean, says his name **O** as in **o**cean.

 Mr U, The Uniform Man, says his name **U** as in **u**niform.

17

FIRST LETTERS

Downsend Lodge (Rowans), Leatherhead

● INTRODUCING LETTERS TO YOUR CHILD

Don't "drill" your child with the letters and sounds. No-one likes being told. It is much easier to learn and remember things when you find them out for yourself. Instead of "teaching" each sound, casually draw attention to a few: the sound at the start of your name or your child's name; the first letter on the bus stop, or the local store, or the packet of juice.

● A GOOD STARTING POINT

Reading aloud to your child is important. At some stage while sharing the stories in picture books your child will begin to realise that the print is part of this exciting story time. You can ask, "Show me where the writing is." They may have play letters for a magnetic surface, an alphabet picture book or frieze. Let them touch the letters and stroke round them. Gradually draw attention to one or two special letters.

Many pre-school children recognize the initial letter of their name or they may recognize the **P** parking sign. Here is a good starting point. Choose a simple game to explore one letter. Playdough is a good choice.

● GO STEADILY

Once your child is involved with one letter, you are ready to take off. But first reflect a moment. When you had your first driving lesson, you were not using all the techniques to drive through the town in the rush hour. You were taught a little at a time. Your child is about to enter the vehicle of the printed word. Go steadily – your child will show you the pace. Tackling too much too soon can lead to discouragement. Build interest and confidence. It is all too easy to destroy both with best intentions. Letterland should be fun.

Look again at the Letterland Characters chart on pages 10 and 11. Remind yourself of the characters and practise their sounds.

● ENJOY THE FUN

One of the best ways of enjoying Letterland together is to make a game of looking for a character's sound in books, shop signs and road signs. Slowly build up the characters known and always talk about the sound they make. For example, while walking towards a sandpit, 4 year old Mark told me that sand belongs to Sammy Snake. When I asked whether the **sss**pade in it belonged to him as well, he nodded yes. When I asked if **b**ucket did, he chuckled with laughter and said, "No, you've got it wrong." We were just talking together. Letterland should never feel like a lesson – keep it fun!

Let your child explore each new letter through games.

■ FIRST LETTER GAMES

● PLAYDOUGH

Try making letter shapes in playdough. Let your child feel each letter. Let him or her look for them while watching you write their name. Talk about the sound. Use the same relaxed play method that you would adopt when helping children to build with bricks. If they smash the letter to bits, chuckle, help them make it again or just make one for them and ask them if it looks the same. You may choose to make the letter's sound as you squash the modelling material. Remember young children enjoy using all their senses to learn. They need to touch the letters and to feel their shape – as well as say the sound they make.

● LETTERLAND PICTURES

Encourage children to draw and paint pictures to illustrate what they know about each character. Here Kicking King is flying his kite.

Callowbrook First School, Rubery

Write the letter shape for very young children and let them add the details that give it its Letterland character. They can add the face and whiskers to **c** to make Clever Cat or the wheels, head and tail to **m** to make Munching Mike. This picture coding helps them remember the image, the Letterland name and therefore the sound that each character makes. If the letter becomes scribbled out by their colouring, don't worry.

● LETTERLAND AT LUNCHTIME

You can even "talk Letterland" while having a meal. Decide together what you think Lucy the Lamp Lady might like for lunch; **l**ettuce and **l**emonade? Or what Bouncy Ben might like for breakfast; **b**aked **b**eans on **b**rown **b**read? And **b**lackberry **b**uns for tea? There are no wrong answers so long as the word begins with that character's letter.

Sammy Snake loves... what? **S**ausages? **S**weets? **S**paghetti? Does Poor Peter like the **p**eas best, or **l**ollipops? Who would he give lollipops to? Who would like the **c**arrots we are having for lunch? **C**..**c**..**c** carrots. Not Bouncy Ben, but who...? Yes, Clever Cat!

Snatches of this sort of Letterland talk over the days and weeks puts your child in a position to know all the answers, simply by learning to listen carefully to the starting sound in words. This is one of the ways in which Letterland creates motivation. Every child enjoys knowing all the answers – even to questions he or she has never been asked before!

You may need to give hints and help at first. Your best help will be the impressed looks you give your child for knowing so much.

● LETTERLAND TOYS

You can bring building toys into the Letterland theme. What can we build for Bouncy Ben? A **b**ridge, a **b**oat, a **b**ig **b**lue **b**us? For Ticking Tess – a **t**ower? For Fireman Fred – a **f**ire engine?

● LETTERLAND CLOTHES

What would Bouncy Ben wear today? **B**ig **b**oots? And Clever Cat. A **c**osy **c**oat? Who would like to wear your **a**norak? Yes, Annie Apple!

Waterside Infant School, Bishop Storfford

● LETTERLAND GUESSING GAMES

Use ordinary objects around the house. Take a tray. Put three or four things on it beginning with the same sound – a **f**lower, a **f**ork, a toy **f**armer, a picture of a **f**ish. Ask "Guess whose this is?" or "Who in Letterland begins **fff**lower?" Later on you can extend the game to include something that does not fit the sound pattern, for example, a **p**en, a **p**encil, a **p**otato and a **l**emon and see if your child can find the odd one out.

If necessary give help, because success ensures a wish to play the same game again another day! Continue to invent the fun. There's no end to the story and play element of Letterland.

Wherever you are, your voice is with you. So you can talk about the Letterland people and their sounds anywhere.

You can make car journeys less tedious by finding, for example, Munching Mike words. Look for the objects out of the window or think of some inside the car – **M**ummy, **m**e, **m**achine, **m**ap. Or play Letterland "I Spy", looking for words beginning with Ticking Tess's sound.

You can play the game the other way round by asking your child to guess which Letterlander begins a particular word. Stick to the letter sounds you can prolong, at first, so young ears can't miss them. They are:

a, **f**, **h**, **i**, **l**, **m**, **n**, **o**, **r**, **s**, **u**, **v**, **w**, **y**, **z**.

Children playing with homemade puppets

LETTERLAND DRESSING UP

Children love dressing up. Let them dress up as a Letterland character. Children like to improvise, so paper ears on a headband, or paper hats and crowns can transform them within moments to Bouncy Bens, cats, puppies, ladies, kings and queens and more.

You can contribute by asking your dressed-up character, "What sound do you say now that you are... ?" Children may extend it to searching through the toy box to find things that start with "their" sound.

LETTERLAND PUPPETS

If you enjoy sewing or knitting you can make finger or glove puppets of some Letterland people and animals.

LETTERLAND MAKE BELIEVE GAMES

Encourage the awareness of letter sounds by inventing sentences and funny stories. Playing "hurrying home with huge steps like the Hairy Hat Man" may create a bit of amusement for onlookers, but will speed up a journey and reinforce a sound!

LETTERLAND FLASHCARDS

Make up games using everyday words written on stiff card. When making these cards remember good clear letter shapes are important. Don't use capital letters except for the word **I** and for the beginning of names. Start with the words **I see** and the names of members of the family or pets. Your child will probably ask for more as the need arises. I made a postman's tabard and cap for a young pre-schooler and gave her an old shoulder bag. Instantly she was a familiar postman. She delivered the name cards to the people in her family. Sometimes she made stories by putting 'I see' before 'mummy' or 'daddy'. Some days later I was telephoned by this little postman with a request for more words. "I need 'love' and 'need' the voice told me. When I asked why, she told me she wanted to make 'I love Mummy and Daddy' and 'I need mummy.' Our postperson was learning the power of print. She was oblivious of the fact that she was taking a big step towards reading. To her it was just an absorbing game.

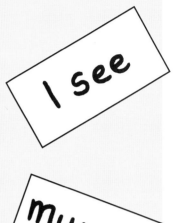

LETTERLAND SCRAPBOOK

Encourage your child to keep a scrapbook. He or she could paste in photographs of items in magazines to give to each character – or places where they might live or visit, or items that might belong to them.

■ READING TO YOUR CHILD

There is immense value to sharing stories and looking at books together. This alone will teach your child a variety of skills.

●...An ability to listen and concentrate for increasing periods of time.

●...A wider vocabulary as your child hears and understands new words in the stories.

●...Confident use of these new words in conversation.

●...Use of his/her imagination, stimulated by each story.

Your child will also learn important basic information.

●...Books have a start and an end, a front page and a back page.

●...The pages of a book are turned one at a time.

●...Print goes from left to right, starting at the top left.

●...Letters and print are linked to words.

●...Words make up sentences. Books will help him or her outgrow the immature "me playing car" type of statement and lead towards "I'm playing with my car."

●...Books are interesting and full of exciting experiences and information.

As adults, we assume that a child will know these things. As a teacher, I have come across some children who have no understanding of how books work and who are unaware that stories are worth listening to. Your child will be more ready for school as a result of this enjoyable sharing of books. Time-consuming? Yes, but worth every minute of it.

Choose an inviting book. Read and look at it together. Make it fun,

then story books will become as important as any other play material in your home. Involve other family members where possible, again keeping it fun.

Go to the library and let your child choose a book. Talk about the pictures, tell the story. Teach very young children to handle books carefully. Give them a special book-shelf so that their books can be put away safely.

Young children love the repetition of the same story over and over again. This is good. They are acquiring ideas, building up their understanding of words and their own ability to listen.

Follow the print with your finger. You are showing the child where the story is. Avoid hiding the picture or the print when you use this finger method. Don't use it all the time. Your teaching needs to be with a very light touch.

Take advantage of the natural breaks in the story to talk about the pictures and to allow the child to dwell on them.

Draw attention to a few words. Talk about the word beginning with Clever Cat's sound if it begins with **c**, or the Hairy Hat Man's sound if it begins with **h**. Look for the words again. Don't learn the alphabet names. When it comes to learning to read they are useless. "Aee, bee, cee" should be introduced later, not now.

Children soon learn to recognise a few words, and this in itself builds their confidence.

"In almost all the schools where the children's progress was good, there were signs that parents took an active interest in helping them to read at home."

The Reading and Hearing of Reading in Primary Schools 1991 – H.M.I. Report

FORMING THE LETTERS

Very young children need to be shown how to form the letter shapes with the correct movements. But how do you describe to a child where to start and finish the letter **d**, for example? It is easy with Letterland. You are describing the movement around Dippy Duck.

"Draw Dippy Duck's back, then go round underneath her tummy, right up to her head and down again."

You can help your child practise writing the strokes which your words describe.

Encourage your child to start the letter in the correct place. The point of starting in the correct place is to teach a style that will lead later on to good, clear, quick cursive (joined-up) writing. An incorrect start may still make a clear, neat shape *but* it will form a habit that will have to be unlearned before your child can develop a cursive style. Old habits are hard to leave behind.

Remember that young children have not yet refined their small hand movements. Your child will come to writing by many large scribbles and many painting sessions. These big uncontrolled movements are part of the learning process.

Copying over a dotted line is quite difficult. First I let young children "feel" the dotted letter with their forefinger several times. Encourage them to start in the correct place and then to make a freehand copy themselves.

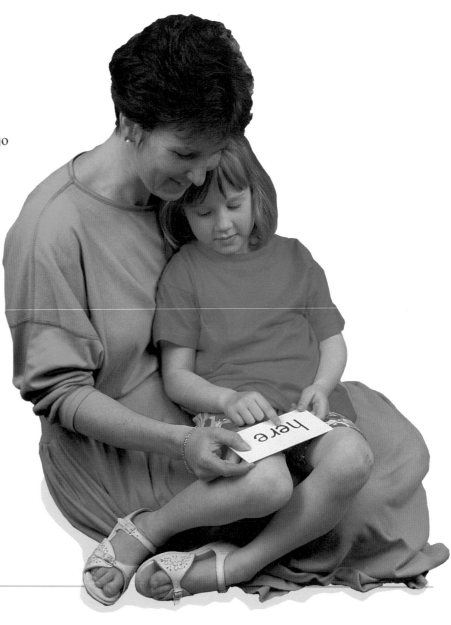

The joy of Letterland is that you can make a boring handwriting line into an interesting experience. How would you tell a child to write **c**? With Letterland you can tell them:

"Start Clever Cat right over by her ear, go over her head, round her face and stop under her chin."

Talk about the Letterland character and make "his" or "her" sound whenever you practice writing it. This talking not only directs the shape of the letter but strengthens the link with its sound.

The young child's concentration span will be short; a few attempts at a single letter will be enough. To make the same letter later on, in the sandpit or on the beach, will be much more fun and just as beneficial. You can even practise writing letter shapes on wet legs in the bath!

Encourage big, controlled, fluid movements rather than tight, tense, small letters. Emphasise the starting place and movement round the shape. Accuracy will come with practice.

In Letterland all the letter characters except **g**, **q** and **z** look the way our eyes move to read print – from left to right.

Refer to letters as "looking in the reading direction." Direction may be a new word. You can add an arrow at the top of the page when you talk about "the reading direction". Your stress on direction will help the child write the letter the correct way round.

These are all ways in which you can help your child in the pre-school years, and you can continue to enjoy Letterland together once your child is at school.

HOW TO FORM

Annie
Apple

Start at the leaf, go round the apple and add a line down.

Bouncy
Ben

Brush down Ben's ears, then go up and around his face.

Eddy
Elephant

Draw a headband across his forehead, then stroke over his head and under his chin.

Fireman
Fred

Start at his helmet, then go down his body. Now give him some arms.

Impy
Ink

Start at the top and make his straight line down. Don't forget to add his dot on top!

Jumping
Jim

Draw down his body and around his knees. Now give him a juggling ball on top.

Munching
Mike

Start at his tail, then give him three legs.

Naughty
Nick

Draw down his nail, then up, over and down again.

Quarrelsome
Queen

Go round her face, then up and down to the end of her hair.

Robber
Red

Go down his body, then up and make his arm.

Uppy
Umbrella

Go down, around and up again. Now draw a straight line down.

Vase of
Violets

Go straight down and straight up.

Yo-Yo
Man

Make the lines for his sack, then draw from his shoulder down to his foot.

THE LETTERS

Clever
Cat

Stroke her from the top of her head, go round her face. Stop under her chin.

Golden
Girl

Start at the top of her swing, go round her head, up and down to the bottom of her swing.

Kicking
King

Go down his body from head to toe. Then give him an arm and a leg.

Oscar
Orange

Start at the top and go all the way round.

Sammy
Snake

Start at his head and stroke down to his tail. Never stroke his scales the wrong way!

Wicked
Water Witch

Straight down and up, then down and up again.

Zig Zag
Zebra

Stroke across her nose, then down her neck, and now across her back.

Dippy
Duck

Start at Dippy Duck's back, then go round her body, up to her head and down.

Hairy
Hat Man

Start at his head. Go down to his heel, then up over his knee and down again.

Lamp
Lady

Go straight down her body from head to toe.

Poor
Peter

Stroke down his long, droopy ear, then up, over his head and round under his chin.

Ticking
Tess

Start at her neck and go down to her toes. Now add her arms.

Max and
Maxine, the
Kissing Cousins

Draw two sticks. Make the second one cross the first.

GENERAL PREPARATION FOR SCHOOL

Don't be over-anxious as your pre-schooler approaches the start of school. It is a major step towards independence, but do not feel that you are losing your child. The influence of a child's home and family is always stronger than the influence of school.

Schools value the support, help and involvement of parents. Share any anxieties you may have with either the head or class teacher, whoever seems more appropriate. Try to avoid sharing anxieties within your child's hearing, whether it be at home or at school. Children can adopt your anxieties or use them to make you feel guilty about leaving them at school. Every reception teacher will have met the child who cries profusely in their parent's presence but is happily playing five minutes after he or she has left.

Don't be surprised if your child does not want to go to school every day. This is the first time that they have met this kind of fixed daily routine. Parents look surprised when I meet a reluctant child with the comment, "Didn't you want to come to school either? Do you know, I felt like staying at home this morning. Let's see if we can find something nice to cheer ourselves up together." The parent may look surprised, but the child identifies with my reluctance and joins me in my search for something to do.

Don't be surprised either if your child seems to be only playing at school.

Throughout this guide I have been encouraging you to "only play" with Letterland. Children who enjoy learning acquire an appetite for it. Just as you are passing on important information about letter shapes and sounds playfully, so your school will be structuring a wide range of learning situations into what the children see as simply "play". Their enjoyment strengthens their learning.

There are practical ways that you can help your child's teacher as well. If Bouncy Ben can do up **b**uttons, could he help your child to try? If Clever Cat can put on a **c**oat, can she encourage your child to do the same? These acts of independence free a teacher and give added teaching time.

Macmillan Nursery School, Plymouth

Fireman Fred at Norfolk Fire Station.

Macmillan Nursery School, Plymouth

LETTERLAND AT SCHOOL

Once your child is at school, you can still participate in your child's learning experience. Letterland helps wherever the printed word is used, whether in a story book, in a reading scheme book, in a newspaper or on a shop sign. Even fluent readers refer to it occasionally as a reading aid and often continue to rely on it to help their spelling.

Merland Rise First School, Epsom

■ SOUNDS IN WORDS

● STARTING SOUNDS AS CLUES

Once at school, your child will learn all the Letterland characters' names and how to use their starting sounds as clues when reading words. Many parents will have said to the hesitant reader, "What does it start with?" Your child's Letterland teacher may say, "Who starts the word?" or help by saying, "Ah, that's Dippy Duck, isn't it, and her sound is… ?" You may like to use the same style of helping. Suggest looking for other clues as well: **do**g and **do**ll both have the same starting pattern, but you can say "Oh, look – two Lamp Ladies at the end saying **ll** together, so that word must be **do**… ?"

● MIDDLE SOUNDS

Middle sounds are harder to hear. Playing brief writing games with words all containing the same vowel sound can help. I have found five or six year olds keen to play at changing a word by changing only one letter. If the game is played with a participating parent or adult, it ceases to be a teaching session and becomes "we are only playing." Take the words **pen**, **peg**, **pet**. All these words start with Poor Peter and Eddy Elephant.

"I write with a…."

"I hang up washing with a …."

"I look after and feed my….."

This writing game should only last for as long as the child wants. It can be played while keeping a child occupied in a doctor's surgery equally well as in the classroom. The child is listening and learning about sounds in words.

● LONGER WORDS AND SYLLABLES

Remember, longer words can be approached comfortably if you encourage your child to look at them in parts. Bet/ter, in/to, milk/man are more accessible to a beginner reader if you reveal the first part or syllable and hide the second part temporarily by a finger. This allows the child to dwell on the first part of the word and then, having worked that out, to add on the second part. Verb endings are very easy to approach in this way. A child who can read **play** will easily cope with **playing** after they have recognised the **play** section. By hiding the **ing** with a finger in the early stages of reading you help your beginner reader to approach the word. Children will remember the **ing** and **ed** endings to words like **play** and they will be more able to reproduce them when spelling **playing** and **played**.

● READING TOGETHER

When reading together, remember to give the child time to work out a word. We can sometimes jump in and supply a word without giving enough time for the child to dwell on it, and to make an attempt at the unfamiliar. But if your child is tired or discouraged, too much waiting can make it feel as though you are testing him or her, instead of keeping reading a pleasure.

If helping your child to recognise letters and their sounds were Letterland's only contribution it would be a useful teaching aid. But Letterland offers much more. It explains 'strange' letter behaviour in a way that makes sense to the child. Examples of this are given on pages 34-39. Your child will be learning that letter behaviour can be exciting and interesting – something they would be unlikely to experience within a traditional phonic teaching programme.

STORIES NOT RULES

Children can easily be confused in reading English. A single letter can make a variety of sounds, and certain letters get together to make completely new sounds!

● SAME LETTER, DIFFERENT SOUNDS

With traditional phonic teaching there are confusing variations which make no sense to a child. For example, hard "cee" is for **c**at, **c**aravan, **c**ar; but soft "cee" is for **c**entre, **c**ircle and **c**ylinder. "Cee-aitch" is for **ch**eese and **ch**ocolate but behaves differently in **Ch**ristmas. These are phonic facts that have to be learned – but they do not have to be learned as dry rules.

● STORY EXPLANATIONS

Letterland replaces rules with brief stories which entertain while they teach. Some of these stories may seem far-fetched, but tell me, which does your child remember more easily: a rule – or a story?

As people we behave towards other people in a variety of ways. For example, I can speak precisely and behave conventionally when meeting other adults. I can chat informally with my friends. At other times I can romp through a wood with a child inventing creepy crawlies and creepy words, having as much fun as that child. I am always being myself but I am showing different aspects of my personality to the different people I am with.

The characters who live in Letterland behave in just this way. They remain themselves but show different behaviour in different situations. So when Letterland provides a story telling why they act differently each time they make a new sound, the system is simply drawing parallels with real life. That is why children feel so much at home in Letterland.

● CLEVER CAT AND THE HAIRY HAT MAN

Let us look at the "cee" sound – Clever Cat's sound. Why is the sound different in **ch**eese or **ch**ocolate? Here we can see Clever Cat right next to the Hairy Hat Man. What is happening now?
The Letterland story explains how his hairy hat makes Clever Cat's nose tickle. So when we see her letter and his letter side by side we hear her sneeze, **ch**! By play-acting being Clever Cat beside the Hairy Hat Man, the children make this new information their own. By introducing a fable-like logic, the Letterland stories make sense of what otherwise seem to be a bewildering number of irregularities.

STRANGE BEHAVIOUR

Letterland is also used in my classroom to introduce children to spelling and to encourage them to look at all the parts of words.

● POOR PETER & THE HAIRY HAT MAN

One day I was revising the letter **p** with some five year olds. We were trying to match some labels to a collection of things that we had found which started with Poor Peter's sound. Christopher called out, "There's a Poor Peter in my name." "Is there?" I responded. The class looked disbelieving: Christopher was not renowned for being right. He collected his clearly labelled tin of crayons and said, "Look – there it is." "Oh, yes. I can see it," I replied but then I asked, "Can you hear it?" He said his name quietly to himself; he repeated it looking very puzzled and then said, "No, but it's there." "Oh, yes," I said. "It's there and you are right, you can't hear it. Would you like to know why?"

I then showed the children the card for **ph** and told the Letterland story. Stated very briefly, whenever Poor Peter meets the Hairy Hat Man in a word the Hat Man turns his head to take a **ph**otogra**ph** of Poor Peter. The story made sense to the children. Now they could all understand the spelling of Christo**ph**er. So when we made a Poor Peter words display, we saved a corner of the display area for a **ph** collection that held a **ph**otogra**ph** and Christo**ph**er's name label. I had not planned to introduce this sound at this point, but Christopher needed to know.

Without Letterland how could I have explained to a group of five year olds the **ph** sound without causing confusion between **p** and **f**?

● NEW LETTER PATTERNS

It is best to explain strange behaviour in letters when the child notices and wants to know. Often the better strategy in the meantime is to look at the meaning of the sentence as a whole for clues to the unfamiliar word. Teaching an atypical letter pattern can wait. Your child will meet it later, perhaps when needing to spell a particular word. That is the best time to learn the story.

Ideally, your child should be telling *you* the stories learnt at school, sure that you will want to know and will appreciate their importance. Retelling the story will help your child to remember it, so your appreciative listening has more than an encouraging function. You will also be keeping in step with the school's timing for each story. Parents who rush ahead of the school's timing can produce bored or know-all pupils who kill the magic of Letterland in the teacher's hands.

This book does not aim to cover all the story explanations which Letterland provides for the many 'wrinkles' in the English language. It does aim to make sure that you and your child can feel confident that there *are* explanations at a *child's* level of understanding.

For advice on how best to answer your child's questions on strange letter behaviour that they have not yet covered in class, see page 44 (Common Problems).

Merland Rise First School, Epsom

■ LETTERLAND STORIES

*Letterland has a story for each new letter combination. For example, the stories explain why two vowels together make a new sound: why you never see **v** at the end of a word on its own but always propped up by **e**; why **y** makes a new sound at the end of words. Each entertaining story catches the child's imagination. The following is a short sample to show how the stories make language come alive.*

● THE HAIRY HAT MAN AND FRIENDS

The Hairy Hat Man has an interesting effect on many Letterland characters. Here are summaries of just three of the story explanations.

ch Clever Cat's nose tickles beside the Hat Man because of his hairy hat. So she sneezes and we hear "**ch**!"

sh The Hairy Hat Man hates noise. Sammy Snake's hissing sound is too noisy so the Hairy Hat Man hushes Sammy up: "**sh**!"

ph The Hairy Hat Man takes a **ph**otogra**ph** of Poor Peter whenever they meet in a word.

Children remember these changes in sound when they learn them as stories.

If your child paints any pictures of **ch**, **sh** or **ph** for you, or other letter combinations learnt at school, hang them around the house. They could picture code labels to stick on the furniture or doors – constant reminders of these "new" sounds.

● THE VOWEL MEN

● Mr A

a Annie Apple belongs to the owner of the **a**pples, Mr A, the Apron Man who collects apples in his **a**pron.

He says **a** as in **a**pron.

● Mr E

e Eddy Elephant belongs to Mr E, the Easy Magic Man, who teaches his pet **e**lephant tricks.

He says **e** as in **e**asy.

● Mr I

Least likely, but dearly loved and understood by the children:-

i Impy Ink belongs to Mr I, the Ice Cream Man, who sells both **i**nk and **i**ce cream!

He says **i** as in **i**ce.

● Mr O

o Oscar Orange belongs to Mr O, the Old Man, who brings **o**ranges from **o**ver the **o**cean.

He says **o** as in **o**cean.

● Mr U

u Uppy Umbrella belongs to Mr U the Uniform Man, who looks after all the **u**mbrellas in Letterland.

He says **u** as in **u**niform.

In traditional phonic teaching, each vowel has both a short and a long sound. In Letterland every vowel has its own Vowel Man.

Remember these long and short vowel sounds can be found both at the beginning and inside words. Do not assume that a capital letter vowel is always the long sound.

The Vowel Men are very important in Letterland. They explain the long vowel sound so easily. Perhaps you remember parroting the 'silent **e**' rule from your school days. This is a very difficult principle to get across as a dry rule. In Letterland terms the rule becomes an intriguing little story which play acting helps to make unforgettable. Mr E, the Easy Magic Man, has invented the silent magic **e** which we so often find at the end of words. That magic will make any of the other Vowel Men pop out and say his name. So the moment you add a silent **e** to **tap** it becomes **tape**, **cub** becomes **cube**, **rid** becomes **ride**, and so on.

Mr. E. the easy magic man

Macmillan Nursery School, Plymouth

● THE ROBBER GANG

There are robbers in Letterland. Whenever a robber appears in a word after a vowel, that vowel's sound will have been stolen! We have met Robber Red. In due course your child will meet a gang of five vowel-stealing robbers who make their own special sounds in words. Any child who learns their sounds, and becomes sharp-eyed enough to catch these robbers at work will find that many difficult words become easy to read.

ar **Ar**thur **Ar** who has a get-away c**ar** to contain the apples he steals.

or **Or**vil **Or** carries an oar with him and steals oranges. He keeps his get-away boat by the sh**or**e.

er Then there are the three robbers we call the **Er** broth**er**s, for that is the sound they make in words.

er Ernest Er (as in broth**er**)

ir Irving Ir (as in f**ir** tree)

ur Urgent Ur (as in f**ur** boots)

The timing for teaching these Letterland stories is important. Teachers are trained to assess and anticipate young readers' needs. To produce too many stories (in effect, to attempt to teach too many rules too soon) can confuse children.

Help your child by <u>not</u> passing on ahead of time any advanced stories that you may have picked up from older children. Remember that very young readers pick up many words by sight memory alone. Don't intrude on this process. For further advice on how best to tackle your child's questions on strange letter behaviour, see page 44.

Arthur **Ar**

Orvil **Or**

Ernest **Er**

Irving **Ir**

Urgent **Ur**

Whitehouse Common First School, Birmingham

■ READING WITH A SCHOOL CHILD

Learning to read is hard work for many children. Often one of the biggest hurdles to overcome is their own lack of confidence. This often comes out as a reluctance even to try. This is frustrating for parent and teacher alike so the most important thing a parent can do is inspire enthusiasm.

● FAMILY READING

Making reading part of the family routine is the best way to encourage children who are not natural reading enthusiasts. Reading together should be an enjoyable time, so choose books that both of you can enjoy. Take time to talk about the story.

At first you will be doing all the reading and your child will be the listener. At this stage it is important that you read steadily, following the printed words with your finger. The print and spoken words become linked in the child's mind.

Soon your child will begin to join in with this reading time. Many parents feel at this stage that their children are merely memorising the story. However, they also pick up some of the words by sight and link them to the print on the page.

● INTRODUCING WORDS

At this stage you can draw their attention to a few words. Take the word "Hello" for instance. They can see its obvious pattern and shape. They can see and hear that it starts with H – Hairy Hat Man doing a handstand!. Does "Hello" turn up again on another page? A few days later remind them of the word "Hello" and see if they can find it in the same book again.

The length of each reading will vary, depending on the child's concentration. Be aware of low interest and stop when your child has had enough.

● SHARED READING

After a few months at school many children are ready to take part and share some of the reading. They will be recognizing some words which crop up often. Encourage their participation and begin to invite them to read to you. Be ready to supply difficult unknown words.

Remember that with some books a shared reading time is quite taxing. Never let your child struggle so that the sense of the story is lost. Sometimes it may be a good idea, part way through the book, for you to take over all the reading.

● PAIRED READING

Some schools adopt a paired reading approach. The reading child is linked to an older child or a parent. Each partner signals to the other when the other partner is ready to take part in the reading. The signal can be a hand squeeze or the words "your turn". If your child's school uses this system you will be advised about it. Some reluctant readers can be encouraged to participate if you adopt this signal system at home.

When your child misreads a word don't immediately correct it. If the incorrect word makes sense, leave it. If the misread word makes no sense, try suggesting various strategies – "Look at the starting sound" or "Remember the **hhh** sound the Hairy Hat Man makes?". This may be enough to stimulate self-correction along with the clues which the sentence context and pictures provide. If not, simply supply the word.

● SOUNDING OUT WORDS

Don't ask a child to attempt to build up each separate sound in a word if that word has more than three letters. Remember that Letterland characters behave differently with each other. For this reason, and because it is difficult to retain the sound blending of more than a few letters, it is easier to help the child to look at a significant part of the word using Letterland clues.

For example, if a child stumbled on the word **middle**, I would explain that the letters **m-i-d** make the sound **mid**. Then I would ask the child to re-read the sentence. Once you have given the start of the word, the picture and story clue will help to indicate the rest of the word.

This method leads a child towards word building. As they learn more Letterland stories and 'sound clues', children are able to combine this with story-sense clues. Both need to develop together to enable a child to move towards being a fluent reader.

● THE BENEFITS OF READING

Reading should not be an activity for its own sake. The message, be it story or fact, is the important element. Make sure that your child has absorbed what has been read, but do so gently by inviting comments rather than by a cross-questioning method.

And when your child is able to read with some fluency, don't stop reading to him or her. Move on to more adventurous books, even if you think the language used in some stories is too advanced or rather old-fashioned. Remember it will help enormously to build your child's vocabulary. Just by listening, children learn about sentence structure, and word meanings, and they absorb the ideas and experiences you are describing.

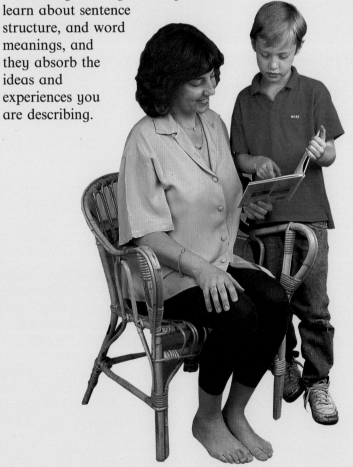

■ SPELLING

The teaching of reading and writing are closely linked. I encourage children to try spelling words even if they make mistakes.

Letterland gives a child a way of talking about letters that is more meaningful than rule talk. Young writers often ask me to confirm their spelling ideas by referring to the Letterland characters. "For **kitchen** is it Clever Cat or Kicking King?" This is fine. The switch to the traditional "aee, bee, cee" terms will happen quite effortlessly as your child progresses at school. Meanwhile the Letterland characters' names avoid many typical confusions between alphabet names and letter sounds.

Letterland offers spelling stories. For example, there are no English words ending with **v**. The Letterland story points out how thin the bottom of the Vase of Violets is. Without support at the end of a word it might topple over! So always add a silent **e** to stop the vase from falling – as in ha**ve**, gi**ve**, lo**ve**.

Children can confuse the positions of **k** and **c** and write **kc** at the end of a word. To them the order may seem random. Letterland gives a reason to establish **ck**. It couldn't be **kc** because Kicking King is a **k**ind **k**ing. He would never kick Clever Cat!

Do not ignore the value of games such as Hangman, Scrabble and simple crosswords. These are excellent spelling activities as well as sociable fun. Take a word like **pen** and try changing one letter at a time. Play the game with a partner and see how many words you can make.

pen

peg

leg

log

lot

pot

You may prefer to limit the game by keeping the middle sound.

pen

peg

leg

let

vet

get

set

Try the same game starting with two consonants.

stop

step

stem

flip

flop

flap

flag

flat

George Palmer Infants, Reading

● SPELLING LISTS

Some children love learning spelling lists: others find them very difficult. The latter group are not necessarily being lazy. They may find it beyond their ability to retain and reproduce these many random patterns of letters. But spelling lists can be an easy way of learning if the words use similar beginnings, middles or endings, and especially if they reinforce a particular Letterland story rule. For example, all the words on these two lists follow the Letterland story that explains "when two vowel men go out walking, the first one usually does the talking."

b**oa**t	s**ai**l
c**oa**t	sn**ai**l
m**oa**t	tr**ai**n
m**oa**n	p**ai**n
gr**oa**n	g**ai**n

Whitehouse Common First School, Birmingham

■ WRITING

Involve your child in writing for a purpose. You could say, "Be my writing hand while I wash up. We need to make a shopping list. Here, you just write down who in Letterland begins the word." Another time you might explain why you need not only Jumping Jim's letter but also a few more letters in **je**lly so you won't buy **ju**nk food or **ju**ice instead by mistake. Never mind if you get **jle** at this stage. Just say cheerfully, "That looks nearly right, we can check it out on the label when we buy it."

Show how to write your address, perhaps linking it with sending away for some novelty or free gift. Help your child to start a scrapbook adding a few words under the pictures. If you can include photographs you will be making this a very special book.

Even letter writing can be exciting when you give your child a stamp and let him or her post the letter.

Don't worry if letters are posted with **b**'s and **d**'s written backwards. Just quietly find ways to practise these letters later. Paint and picture code them. Do the same for any other difficult letter or word. Plaster bedroom or even bathroom walls with them.

Letterland is the friendliest aid I know for teaching correct letter formation. Look at the chart on forming letters on page 28. If your child makes the letter using the incorrect movement around the shape, tell him or her what they are doing to the Letterland shape. For example, "Help! You'll ruffle Dippy Duck's feathers that way!" This gives you both a reason to laugh – much more memorable and encouraging than the adult saying "That's wrong. You must start with the circle and then do the stick."

■ COMMON PROBLEMS

● READING

Your child is stuck on a word while reading to you. Do you supply it?

Yes, in the very early stages of reading – but after that vary it. Sometimes hold back a while and give your child a chance to think it through. The story sense and picture may be sufficient to help find the word. Or help with a hint. Never let the wait become painfully long.

Do you sound out words letter by letter?

Only the first three letters. This may be enough to trigger the word. With longer words, help your child put two consonant sounds together, **st**, **dr**, **fl**, if they are trying to pronounce them separately.

Your child misreads a word. What do you do?

If the misread word makes sense, leave it. If it is a senseless misread, invite the child to look at it again and then re-read that part of the story. If confidence is low, you re-read up to the difficult word and maybe supply the first syllable.

Your child is puzzled by a Letterland combination and you do not know the explanation.

Tell your child that there must be a special Letterland story to explain it. Maybe wonder aloud about the explanation. Letterland always finds one. Make a note of it and mention it to your child's teacher. This will strengthen the school/home link. Once the teacher is aware that this combination has interested the child, he or she may decide to explain the story behind it at that point, or later with the rest of the class. Remind your child that you would like to learn the story, too.

Your child does not want to read at all.

Buy or borrow from the library an interesting book and don't read it to your child. When a friend calls to play, casually offer to show and read it to the friend! This will often be enough to tempt the uninterested child.

● WRITING

When writing, your child often reverses a letter or letters.

Draw attention to the picture coding and practise making the letter together. Try finger paints. Gently ask your child whether the letter is looking the right way. Remember, all but 3 of the Letterland letters look in the reading direction (see page 10).

Your child loves writing but has no spelling sense at all.

Let them have their own private diary to satisfy their need to write without anyone correcting them. Ask for and give simple messages, writing out the correct spelling of one or two common words at a time.

Talk to your teacher. The kind of errors your child makes can help in deciding how you can help most constructively.

● SPEECH

Your child's speech is 'lazy'.

Children write as they talk, so lazy speech can be reproduced in spelling. "I atto go out," "Me bruvver plays wiv me." Be sensitive in your approach. I smile encouragingly and over-emphasise the sound to be made, letting the child watch my mouth and lips making the shape. "Now you try." Make this a game you play when the child is happy and relaxed. Do not expect immediate improvement. Use Letterland characters to remind your child of the correct pronunciation. Children don't step in a "puggle" when you can tell them that Dippy Duck and her friend want to make their sound in the middle of the "pu**dd**le". You could make a 'Spelling Picture' of the word together and playfully say, "Hello ducks in the puddle" each time you pass it on the wall.

A child who has been mispronouncing a word for a long time may need quite a bit of practice to shift out of that well-established habit. If you think that your child's speech is not developing properly, consult your Health Authority Speech Therapy Unit. Many speech therapists use Letterland characters to talk about letters and sounds.

Your child stammers.

A stammering child needs special help, so consult a speech therapist. Avoid answering for your child; over protection can hinder a child's development. Stammers are easiest to overcome when attended to early on.

■ THE NATIONAL CURRICULUM

Until 1988 every state school in England and Wales was free to choose which subjects they taught – and how they taught them. They selected their own curriculum. But the 1988 Education Act laid down that schools must abide by certain national guidelines and adopt the National Curriculum.

■ KEY STAGES

The National Curriculum covers 4 age groups or Key Stages. Children aged up to 7-plus come under Key Stage 1.

■ ASSESSMENT

At the end of each Key Stage all children are assessed. This is done in two ways. The first part is the teacher's continuous assessment of progress made throughout each year of schooling and the second part is based on the children's performance in the Standard Assessment Tasks or SATs. These are very much like their ordinary school work. In fact, many schools report that the 7 year olds were unaware they were being 'tested'.

The results of the continuous assessment and the SATS are combined to reach the final grading. As a parent, you will be informed of the results of these assessments.

■ ATTAINMENT TARGETS

Each curriculum subject is divided into four or five areas or Attainment Targets. In English the Targets for 5-7 year olds are:

Speaking and listening, Reading, Writing, Spelling and Handwriting.

■ LEVELS

The work done in each Attainment Target is graded into 10 different levels covering the whole 5 to 16 age group. Level 1 is the simplest and represents the level of work carried out by 5 year olds.

Level 2 would be the grade achieved by the average child at age 7.

The following is a selection of examples of what is expected of pupils at Key Stage 1 in English.

● SPEAKING & LISTENING

LEVEL 1
Participate as speakers and listeners in group activities, including imaginative play.

LEVEL 2
Listen attentively to stories and poems, and talk about them.

LEVEL 3
Listen with an increased span of concentration to other children and adults, asking and responding to questions and commenting on what has been said.

LETTERLAND HELPS BY
Re-telling Letterland stories; dressing up and play-acting.

Learning Letterland stories, poems and rhyming songs; talking about letter behaviour.

Listening, questioning and discussing the Letterland stories.

Encouraging "why?" questions.

● READING

LEVEL 1
Begin to recognise individual words or letters in familiar contexts.

LEVEL 2
Read accurately and understand straightforward signs, labels and notices.

LEVEL 3
Read aloud from familiar stories and poems fluently and with appropriate expression.

LETTERLAND HELPS BY
Arousing interest in printed letters in books and elsewhere.

Encouraging early familiarity with both capital and small letter shapes.

Providing simple early reading books which encourage beginners.

Enabling children to look for and use phonic clues.

● WRITING

LEVEL 1
Use pictures, symbols or isolated letters, words or phrases to communicate meaning.

LEVEL 2
Produce, independently, pieces of writing using complete sentences, some of them demarcated with capital letters and full stops or question marks.

LEVEL 3
Produce, independently, pieces of writing using complete sentences, mainly demarcated with capital letters and full stops or question marks.

LETTERLAND HELPS BY
Encouraging drawing (bringing the letters to life).

Providing built-in picture clues for both small and capital letter shapes.

Using game-playing to strengthen punctuation.

Generating confidence in early writing through heightened awareness of sound/symbol links.

● SPELLING

LEVEL 1
Write some letter shapes in response to speech sounds and letter names.

LEVEL 2
Produce recognisable (though not necessarily always correct) spelling of a range of common words.

LEVEL 3
Recognise and use correctly regular patterns for vowel sounds and common letter strings.

LETTERLAND HELPS BY
Offering a huge support at all three levels.

Teaching spelling patterns.

Explaining both regular and 'strange' letter behaviour.

Fostering confident attempts at spelling words not previously met.

● HANDWRITING

LEVEL 1
Begin to form letters with some control over the size, shape and orientation of letters or lines of writing.

LEVEL 2
Produce legible upper and lower case letters in one style.

LEVEL 3
Begin to produce clear and legible joined-up writing.

LETTERLAND HELPS BY
Enabling the teacher, parent and child to talk about letter shape, formation and direction without confusion.

Giving the child a memorable image to follow when forming letter shapes. "Draw down Poor Peter's ear, back up and over his head and stop under his chin. Rest his chin on the writing line."

Providing a careful transition stage for semi-joined up writing, followed by a full joined-up handwriting programme.

■ CHILDREN TEACH YOU

Children enter into the imaginary realm of Letterland far more than we ever can. Let them teach you. Invite them to tell you what they have learned about Letterland. Children love to be the teachers.

The parents of children that I have taught are only too well aware of my mannerisms and oddities. They see their child imitating me all too often. Let your child be your teacher about odd letter behaviour. Let him or her feel you rely on them to keep you informed. Instead of them always having to look to you for information, you look to them! They will thrive on the reversed roles.

Without your child you would not have entered Letterland. Please continue to share its fun.

Let's Play

TRADITIONAL GAMES
OF CHILDHOOD

First published in Canada in 1995 by
Kids Can Press Ltd,
29 Birch Avenue,
Toronto, Ontario, Canada,
M4V 1E2

This edition published in Great Britain in 1997
by Heinemann Children's Reference,
an imprint of Heinemann Educational Publishers,
Halley Court, Jordan Hill, Oxford, OX2 8EJ,
a division of Reed Educational & Professional Publishing Ltd.

MADRID ATHENS PARIS
FLORENCE PORTSMOUTH NH CHICAGO
SAO PAULO SINGAPORE TOKYO
MELBOURNE AUCKLAND IBADAN
GABORONE JOHANNESBURG KAMPALA NAIROBI

British Library Cataloguing in Publication Data

Gryski, Camilla
    Let's play : traditional games of childhood
    1. Games - Juvenile literature
    I. Title II. Gryski, Camilla III. Petričić, Dušan
    790.1'922

    ISBN 0431045941

Printed in Hong Kong by Wing King Tong Company Limited